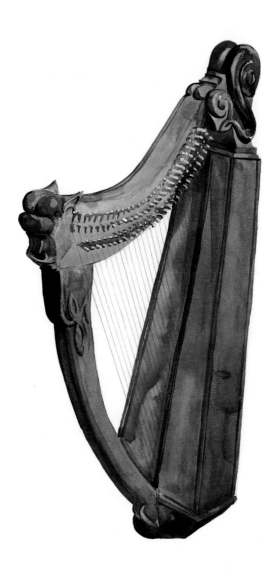

THE
FESTIVE FOOD
OF
IRELAND

Darina Allen

ILLUSTRATED BY SALLY MALTBY
PHOTOGRAPHS BY KEVIN DUNNE

ROBERTS RINEHART PUBLISHERS

Published in Ireland by
Roberts Rinehart Publishers
3 Bayview Terrace
Schull, West Cork
First published in Great Britain by
Kyle Cathie Limited

Published in the United States by
Roberts Rinehart Publishers
P.O. Box 666
Niwot, Colorado 80544

ISBN 1 879373 37 8

Library of Congress Catalog Card Number
92-85180

Designed by Geoff Hayes
Colour origination by Daylight Colour Art Pte. Ltd.
Printed in Hong Kong by
Colorcraft Ltd.

A **roux** is required in some recipes to thicken
sauces; to make this, melt 110g/4oz/1stick butter in
a saucepan, stir in 110g/4oz/1cup flour and cook
gently for 2 minutes, stirring occasionally. Use as
required; the roux can be stored in the refrigerator
for two weeks, or made up on the spot.

Contents

St Bridget's Day

St Bridget is the much-loved Irish saint from early Christian times whose feast day is celebrated on February 1. Originally this was the Celtic festival Imbolc celebrating the first day of spring and the beginning of the new year on the farm.

Bridget is portrayed as a warm-hearted, charismatic woman – a latter day liberated lady in the best sense of the word. She was influential, travelled widely, entertained with panache and was known for her kindness to people and animals.

Bridget is the patron saint of cattle and dairy work, and her cows are said to have produced more and better milk than any other herd. She is also reputed to have been the best mead and ale maker in Ireland. She also loved to cook – and like many saints she could feed the multitude with very little.

Various traditions were associated with Bridget's Day. In some parts of the country a 'stron' of oaten bread in the shape of a cross was baked on St Bridget's Eve and put out on the windowsill together with a sheaf of straw for the saint and her pet white cow, so that she would bless the house. Right to this day children all over the country are shown how to make little crosses from rushes, which they hang up proudly in their homes. It was also the custom to put out a strip of cloth or ribbon called the *Brat Bhride*, Bridget's mantle, for the saint to touch. This would have curative powers.

In many parts of Connacht and Munster groups of young people dress up in colourful garb with ribbons, sashes, masks and fancy straw hats and go from house to house carrying a straw doll dressed in white called the *Brideog*. The 'Biddies' or 'Biddy Boys' play music on concertinas and tin whistles and sometimes sing and dance. In return they are usually given sweets, biscuits and a little money.

Boxty Pancakes

Boxty was traditionally eaten with freshly churned butter on St Bridget's Day.

serves 4–6
225g/8oz freshly cooked potatoes
225g/8oz peeled raw potatoes
225g/8oz/2cups white flour
½teaspoon/¼teaspoon bicarbonate of soda
225–350ml/8–12fl oz/1–1½cups buttermilk
pinch of salt (optional)
butter for frying

1 Peel the cooked potatoes while still hot and mash in a bowl.
2 Grate the raw potatoes and add to the mash with the sieved flour and soda. Add salt if desired.
3 Mix well and add enough buttermilk to make a stiff batter.
4 Heat a frying-pan, grease with butter and cook large or small pancakes in the usual way.
5 Eat the pancakes straight from the pan with butter, crispy rashers or pure Irish honey.

Steak and Oyster Pie

serves 4–6

675g/1½lb best quality beef (round steak, best
  chuck or thick rib steak)
15–30g/½–1oz/⅛–¼ stick butter
225g/8oz onions, chopped
1tablespoon/1½tablespoons white flour
575ml/1pint/2½cups homemade beef stock
225g/8oz/scant 2½cups mushrooms, sliced
12 native or Gigas oysters
roux if necessary
salt and freshly ground pepper
255g/9oz puff, flaky or rough puff pastry
egg wash

1 Cut the beef into 4cm/1½inch cubes and season
with salt and pepper.
2 Melt a little of the butter in a deep frying-pan and
seal the meat over a high heat. Remove to a plate.
3 Add the onions to the pan and cook for 5–6
minutes.
4 Add the flour, stir and cook for 1 minute, blend in
stock, add the meat, bring to the boil, transfer to a
casserole, cover and simmer on a low heat or cook
in a 150°C/300°F/gas2 oven for 1½–2 hours.
5 Meanwhile, sauté the mushrooms in the rest of
the butter in a very hot pan, season with salt and
pepper, keep aside. Open the oysters and put in a
bowl with their juice.
6 When the meat is tender thicken the gravy slightly
with roux if necessary. Add the mushrooms, oysters
and their juice to the stew and taste for seasoning.
7 Allow to cool, put into a pie dish, cover with
pastry, flute the edges and decorate the top. Brush
with egg wash and cook in a preheated 230°C/
450°F/gas8 oven for 10 minutes, then reduce the
heat to 190°C/375°F/gas5 and cook for a further 15–
20 minutes or until the pastry is puffed and golden.

St Patrick's Day

St Patrick is the patron saint of Ireland, responsible, we are told, for converting the pagan Irish to Christianity. He used the shamrock to illustrate how three separate leaves united by one stem resembled the Trinity. To this day the shamrock, the emblem of Ireland, is proudly worn on March 17.

Patrick's Day, Ireland's principal feast day, came as a welcome break during Lent in the days of austere fasting. As children we were all expected to 'give up' something for Lent. Our beloved sweets and sticky toffee bars were the most obvious if reluctant choice and any that came our way were carefully hoarded so we could have a mighty feast on St Patrick's Day.

Children still wear little green badges and the girls sport green ribbons in their hair. In many parts of the country people go to a *ceili* of traditional Irish dancing in the evening. Men who 'take the pledge' and forswear alcohol for Lent (still a surprisingly common occurence) often celebrate on the feast day by drinking the *Pota Padraig*. St Patrick's Day is celebrated by Irish people both at home and abroad. In farflung corners of the world the Irish come together on this day to tuck in to corned beef and cabbage or boiled bacon and cabbage, the traditional emigrants' meal.

12

Corned Beef and Cabbage

Although this dish is rarely eaten nowadays in Ireland, for Irish-Americans it conjures up powerful nostalgic images of a rural Irish past. Originally it was a traditional Easter Sunday dinner. The beef killed before the winter would have been salted and could now be eaten after the long Lenten fast with fresh green cabbage and floury potatoes.

serves 6–8
1.8kg/4lb corned silverside of beef or boiled
   Irish bacon
3 large carrots, cut into large chunks
6–8 small onions, roughly chopped
1teaspoon dry English mustard
large sprig of fresh thyme and some parsley stalks
1 cabbage
salt and freshly ground pepper

1 Put the corned beef or boiled bacon into a saucepan with the carrots, onions, mustard powder and the herb bunch.
2 Add enough cold water to immerse the meat, bring to the boil and simmer, covered, for 1 hour.
3 Discard the outer leaves of the cabbage, cut in quarters and add to the pot. Cook for a further 1–2 hours or until the meat and vegetables are tender.
4 Serve the corned beef or boiled bacon cut into slices surrounded by the vegetables, with lots of floury potatoes and mustard as an accompaniment.

Porter Cake

This fruit cake is made with the famous black stout of Ireland. Its distinctive flavour makes it a great favourite – so much so that it is even exported in tins to Irish emigrants in the United States.

225g/8oz/2sticks butter
225g/8oz/1½cups brown sugar
300ml/½pint/1¼cups stout,
    Guinness or Murphy
zest of 1 orange
225g/8oz/1cup sultanas
225g/8oz/1cup raisins
110g/4oz/½cup mixed peel
450g/1lb/4cups plain white
    flour
½teaspoon bicarbonate of soda
2 teaspoons mixed spice
110g/4oz/½cup glacé cherries
3 eggs

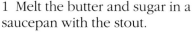

1 Melt the butter and sugar in a saucepan with the stout.
2 Add the orange zest and all the fruit except the cherries. Bring to the boil and boil for 3–4 minutes, stirring frequently. Remove from the heat and allow to cool until lukewarm.
3 Sieve the flour, soda and spice into a mixing bowl. Add the fruit mixture to the flour and then add the cherries.
4 Whisk the eggs and add gradually, mixing well.
5 Spoon the mixture into a prepared 23cm/9inch round tin and bake in the middle of a preheated 180°C/350°F/gas 4 oven for about 1½ hours.
6 If you wish you may pour 4 tablespoons of stout over the cake when it is cooked (prick the cake with a skewer first). Keep for a day before cutting. This cake will keep well for several weeks in a tin.

Easter

Even though Easter is the most important Christian festival the word Easter is linked to the pagan cult of the Saxon goddess of spring, Eostre. The eggs universally associated with Easter are ancient symbols of spring, rebirth and resurrection.

Well, symbolic they may be but it seems to me more likely that the Easter egg tradition is rooted in the ancient custom of Lenten fasting which was common to both Eastern and Western Christendom. The last eggs were eaten up in the form of pancakes on Shrove Tuesday, but as the hens didn't know it was Lent, needless to say they went on laying! The surplus of eggs that accumulated was enjoyed at Easter in all sorts of different ways.

In Ireland, traditionally, some were hard-boiled with natural dyes such as herbs, flowers, lichen or onion skins to colour their shells. Some were preserved by various means: in the Cork area eggs were collected from the nest as soon as they were laid and the shells were rubbed with a thin layer of butter while they were still warm. Buttered eggs are still sold in the English market in Cork city. The eggs laid on Good Friday were considered blessed and these, marked with a cross, were cooked for breakfast on Easter Sunday. Everyone was expected to eat their share of eggs in one form or another and anyone who couldn't manage at least two or three was considered very feeble.

In our house in Shanagarry, County Cork, Easter is always a very exciting time for the children. Preparations begin early. A large wicker basket is lined with sweet hay and decorated with spring flowers. The eggs that are laid on Good Friday are painted with faces and the children's names, and early on Easter Sunday they are slipped back into the nesting boxes in the hen house without letting

out the hens – quite a feat, believe me! Chocolate Easter eggs are mysteriously laid in clumps of daffodils, low shrubs and hedges. The breakfast table is laid with egg cups and fresh soda bread is put into the Aga. As soon as the children wake up they race off to see whether the hens have laid their special Easter eggs. They collect them in a specially decorated and flower-lined wicker basket and bring them into the house to be boiled for breakfast. When these have been gobbled down followed by slices of bread and jam the hunt begins outside for the hidden chocolate treats.

16

Irish Nettle Soup (page 23)

Fadge or Potato Bread (page 31)

Brown Soda Bread and Scones

Brown and white soda breads are widely made in Ireland. Originally they were cooked in an iron bastible or pot oven beside the open fire. They are very fast to make and are best eaten fresh.

675g/1½lb/6cups brown wholemeal flour
  (preferably stone-ground)
450g/1lb/4cups white flour
2teaspoons salt
2teaspoons bicarbonate of soda,sieved
750–900ml/1¼–1⅔pints/3¼–4cups buttermilk

1 Mix together the dry ingredients in a large bowl.
2 Make a well in the centre and add most of the buttermilk. Working from the centre, mix with your hands into a dough, adding more milk if necessary. The dough should be soft but not too sticky.
3 Turn out on to a floured board and pat lightly into a round. Flatten slightly to about 5cm/2inches thick and place on a baking sheet.
4 Mark with a deep cross and bake in a preheated 230°C/450°F/gas8 oven for 15–20 minutes, then reduce the heat to 200°C/400°F/gas6 and bake for a further 20–25 minutes or until the bread is cooked and sounds hollow when tapped.
Note: to make a richer soda bread dough add 30g/1oz fine oatmeal, 1 egg and 30g/1oz butter to the mixture.

Brown Soda Scones

1 Make the dough as above.
2 Form it into a round and flatten to 2½cm/1inch thick round. Stamp out into scones with a cutter or cut with a knife.
3 Bake for about 30 minutes in a hot oven, turning down the oven temperature after 15 minutes, as above.

Easter Egg Nests

Children have great fun making these biscuit nests.

makes 9
225g/8oz/2cups self-raising flour
55g/2oz/½stick butter
1½tablespoons/2tablespoons milk
75g/2½oz/⅓cup caster sugar
½teaspoon pure vanilla essence
1 egg, beaten
1 egg beaten with a pinch of salt to glaze

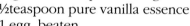

Lemon icing
170g/6oz/1¼cups icing (confectioner's) sugar
grated rind of 1 lemon
2–3tablespoons freshly squeezed
    lemon juice
45–50 mini chocolate eggs
fluffy Easter chickens

1 Sieve the flour into a bowl and rub in the butter.
Make a well in the centre.
2 Put the milk into a small saucepan with the sugar,
add the vanilla essence and stir until the sugar is
dissolved. Add the egg and pour into the well in the
centre of the flour, mix into a stiff dough, and knead
lightly until smooth.
3 Roll out about three-quarters of the dough to
5mm/¼inch thick and stamp out nine rounds with a
7.5cm/3inch cutter. Transfer to a baking sheet.
4 Take 2 walnut-sized pieces of dough and roll into
thin rolls measuring about 13.5cm/5½inches in
length. Twist the two rolls together. Egg-wash the
outside edge of one of the bases and gently press
the rope of dough down on to the base, sealing the
ends. Egg-wash. Carefully repeat with the remaining
dough and bases.

5 Bake in a preheated 180°C/350°F/gas4 oven
for 15–20 minutes or until pale golden.
6 Meanwhile make the icing. Mix the lemon rind
and lemon juice with the sieved icing sugar in bowl.
7 When the biscuits are cooked, cool slightly and
brush with lemon icing, fill with mini chocolate eggs
and decorate each one with a fluffy Easter chick.

Simnel Cake

This traditional Easter cake was introduced to
Ireland centuries ago by English settlers. It has a
layer of almond paste baked into the centre and a
thick layer of almond icing on top and is decorated
with eleven little marzipan balls, representing
eleven of the twelve apostles – Judas is missing
because he betrayed Jesus.

350g/12oz/2 generous cups best-quality sultanas
350g/12oz/1½ generous cups best-quality currants
350g/12oz/1½cups best-quality raisins
110g/4oz/½cup natural glacé cherries, washed and
    chopped
110g/4oz/½cup best-quality candied peel
55g/2oz/scant ½cup whole almonds, skinned
55g/2oz/generous ½cup ground almonds
zest of 1 lemon
zest of 1 orange
60ml/2½fl oz/generous ¼cup Irish whiskey
225g/8oz/2sticks butter
225/8oz/1½cups pale soft brown sugar
6 eggs, beaten
285g/10oz/2¼cups flour
1teaspoon mixed spice
1 large or 2 small Bramley Seedling apples, grated

Almond paste
450g/1lb/4cups ground almonds
450g/1lb/2cups caster sugar
2 small eggs
50ml/2fl oz/¼cup Irish whiskey
a drop of almond essence

1 Line the base and sides of a 23cm/9inch round, or
a 20.5cm/8inch square tin with brown paper and
greaseproof paper.
2 Mix the dried fruit, nuts, ground almonds and
orange and lemon zest. Add the whiskey and leave
for 1 hour to macerate.
3 Meanwhile make the almond paste. Sieve the
sugar and mix with the ground almonds. Beat the
eggs, add the whiskey and 1 drop of pure almond
essence, then add to the other ingredients and mix
to a stiff paste (you may not need all the egg).
4 Sprinkle the work top with icing (confectioner's)
sugar, turn out the almond paste and work lightly
until smooth. Set aside.
5 Cream the butter until very soft, add the sugar and
beat until light and fluffy.
6 Add the eggs bit by bit, beating well between
each addition so that the mixture doesn't curdle.
7 Mix the spice with the flour and fold in gently.
8 Combine the grated apple and the fruit and stir
gently but thoroughly into the cake mixture (don't
beat again or you will toughen the cake).
9 Put half of the cake mixture into the prepared tin.
10 Roll out half the almond paste into a 21.5cm/
8½inch round, place this on top of the cake mixture
in the tin and cover with the remaining mixture.
Make a slight hollow in the centre and dip your
hand in water and pat it over the surface of the
cake: this will ensure that the top is smooth when
cooked.
11 Bake in a preheated 160°C/325°F/gas3 oven for
one hour, then reduce the heat to 150°C/300°F/gas2

and bake for a further two hours, or until the cake is cooked (a skewer inserted in the centre should come out perfectly clean). Leave to cool in the tin.

12 Next day remove the cake from the tin. Do not remove the lining paper but wrap in some extra greaseproof paper and tinfoil until required.

13 When you are ready to ice the cake, roll two-thirds of the remaining almond paste into a 23cm/ 9inch round. Brush the cake with a little lightly beaten egg white and top with the paste.

14 Roll the remaining almond paste into eleven balls about the size of a large walnut. Score the top of the cake in 4cm/1½inch squares and brush with beaten egg or egg yolk. Stick the 'apostles' around the outer edge of the top and brush with beaten egg. Toast under a grill in a preheated 220°C/425°F/gas7 oven, for 15–20 minutes or until slightly golden. (Protect the sides with tin foil.)

15 Decorate with an Easter chicken.

Note: This cake is usually only iced on top but we enjoy the toasted almond paste so much that we like to cover the sides also!

May Day

May Day or Bealtaine is one of the four great Celtic festivals, a celebration of the first day of summer. In many parts of the country it was traditional to light bonfires and to cut and decorate a May bush or pole around which people would dance for a cake until the early hours.

When I was a child my friends and I built May altars or shrines both in the house and the garden in honour of Our Lady, and decorated them with little vases of primroses, bluebells and May bush. We then gathered baskets of young stinging nettles and chased each other with much glee!

The nettles that survived were brought home and made into soup or cooked like spinach. There was, and still is, a very firm belief that nettles should be eaten three times during the month of May to purify the blood after winter and to keep 'the rheumatics' away for another year. Elderflowers are also in bloom in May and we use these to make a magical muscat-flavoured syrup in which to poach the first of the tart green gooseberries.

Irish Nettle Soup

serves 6
45g/1½oz butter
500g/1lb 2oz potatoes
115g/4oz onions
100g/3½oz leeks
1litre/1¾pints/4½cups chicken stock
140g/5oz young nettles, washed
  and chopped
150ml/5floz/¾cup cream or creamy milk
salt and freshly ground pepper

1 Melt the butter in a heavy saucepan; when it foams, add the potatoes, onions and leeks, and toss them in the butter until well coated.
2 Sprinkle with salt and pepper, cover with a paper lid (to keep in the steam) and the saucepan lid, and sweat on a gentle heat for 10 minutes, or until the vegetables are soft but not coloured.
3 Discard the paper lid. Add the stock and simmer until the vegetables are just cooked. Add the nettle leaves and cook until soft; do not overcook or the vegetables will lose their flavour. Add the cream and liquidise. Taste and correct seasoning if necessary. Serve hot.

Poached Salmon with Irish Butter Sauce

Salmon, the king of the Irish river, has been written about endlessly in Irish poems and legends. The season opens on March 17. This is one of the most delicious ways to eat it.

serves 8
900g/2lb centre cut of fresh salmon
salt (use 1 tablespoon of salt to every 1.1litre/2pints
water

23

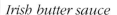

Irish butter sauce
2 egg yolks, free range if possible
2 teaspoons cold water
115g/4oz/1stick Irish butter, cut into dice
1 teaspoon lemon juice
flat parsley, fennel leaves and lemon segments to
  garnish

1 Choose a saucepan that will barely fit the piece of
fish: an oval cast-iron saucepan is usually perfect. (If
a small piece of fish is cooked in a large saucepan of
water, much of the flavour will escape into the
water, so it is important to use the smallest saucepan
possible.)
2 Half fill with salted water and bring to the boil.
Put in the piece of fish, bring back to the boil, cover
and simmer very gently for 20 minutes.
3 Turn off the heat and allow the fish to sit in the
water while you make the sauce (do not let it sit for
more than 20 minutes or so).
4 Put the egg yolks in a heavy stainless steel
saucepan on a low heat, or in a bowl over hot
water. Add the water and whisk thoroughly.
5 Add the butter bit by bit, whisking all the time. As
soon as one piece melts, add the next. The mixture
will gradually thicken, but if it shows signs of
becoming too thick or slightly 'scrambling', remove
from the heat immediately and add a little cold
water. Do not leave the pan or stop whisking until
the sauce is made. If the sauce is slow to thicken it
may be because you are excessively cautious and
the heat is too low. Increase the heat slightly and
continue to whisk until the sauce thickens to coating
consistency.
6 Add lemon juice to taste.
7 Just before serving, skin the salmon and lay it on
a hot serving dish. Garnish with the parsley, fennel
leaves and lemon segments and serve with the Irish
butter sauce.

Carrageen Moss Pudding with Green Gooseberry and Elderflower Compôte

Carrageen moss is a seaweed that grows around the coast of Ireland. During the summer months it is spread out on the grassy cliffs, where it is bleached by the sun and washed by the rain. It is a rich source of iodine and trace elements and a prime source of natural gelatine. *Carrageen* means 'little rock' in Gaelic.

serves 6
8g/¼oz/½cup cleaned, well dried carrageen moss
    (1 semi-closed fistful)
900ml/1⅔pints/4cups milk
½teaspoon pure vanilla essence or a vanilla pod
1 egg, preferably free range
1tablespoon/1½tablespoons caster sugar

1 Soak the carrageen in tepid water for 10 minutes.
2 Strain off the water and put the carrageen into a saucepan with the milk and vanilla pod if used. Bring to the boil, cover and simmer very gently for 20 minutes.
3 At that point and not before, separate the egg and put the yolk in a bowl with the sugar and vanilla essence (if used in preference to vanilla pod). Whisk together for a few seconds, and then pour the milk and carrageen moss through a strainer on to the egg yolk mixture, whisking all the time. The carrageen will now be swollen and exuding jelly.
4 Rub all this jelly through the strainer and whisk it into the milk and egg yolk mixture.
5 Test for a set in a saucer as one would with gelatine. If it doesn't set put a ladleful of the mixture back into the sieve with the carrageen and push more of the jelly through.

outbuildings painted and whitewashed – and inside the house is springcleaned from top to bottom, and even redecorated..

I remember from my childhood that the day before, the parlour table would be covered with an embroidered linen tablecloth and the best china taken down from the dresser or the sideboard. Mass was usually said in the kitchen and the kitchen table was used as an altar. It was covered with a starched linen cloth kept specially for the purpose. On the day itself, fresh flowers were gathered, and adults and children were brushed and dressed up in their finery so that all was in readiness before the parish priest and curate arrived. The woman of the house and one or two friends would have been up since dawn, making final preparations for the breakfast after the Mass. There were fires to be lit, breads to be baked and butter balls to be made from the freshly churned butter.

The neighbours, friends and relatives arrived first, and, as soon as the priests arrived, one began to hear confessions by the fire in the parlour while the other priest began to celebrate Mass and distribute Holy Communion. After Mass the next person to have the Stations would be decided upon and the dues would be collected. The priests would then sit down in the parlour with the assembled company to a breakfast feast of porridge with thick cream followed by a lavish fry-up served with a mountain of buttered toast, soda bread and copious cups of strong tea.

The Stations were officially over when the priests left, but in many parts of the country it was only then that the real social celebration began. Often there would be a sing-song with music on a melodeon or even a few tin whistles. Stories were told and eventually people made their way home with a few sugar lumps as a treat for the children.

An Irish Breakfast

might comprise any or all of the following:

back bacon rashers, green or smoked
streaky bacon rashers, green or
smoked pork sausages
tomatoes
slices of white and black pudding
free range eggs
wild mushrooms if you can get them

Serve with lots of fresh soda bread (see page 17)
and hot toast.

An *Ulster fry* would include fried potato bread or
'fadge' (see opposite) and very delicious it is too.

Pinhead Oatmeal Porridge

McCann's Irish Oatmeal
is the only pinhead
oatmeal available in the
U.S. – and has been sold
there since 1871!

serves 4
150g/5Hoz/scant 1cup
   pinhead oatmeal
900ml/1Npints/4cups water
1 level teaspoon salt

1 Mix the oatmeal in 250ml/
8fl oz/1cup of cold water.
Bring the rest of the water to
the boil and add to the oatmeal.
2 Put on a low heat and stir until
the water comes back to the boil. Cover and simmer
for 30 minutes, stirring occasionally.

3 Stir in the salt, cover again and leave aside overnight – the oatmeal will absorb all the water.
4 Reheat and serve with cream and soft brown sugar.

Fadge or Potato Bread

In Ulster people are passionate about fadge or potato bread. It can be cooked on a griddle, in a frying-pan or in the oven.

serves 8
900g/2lb unpeeled 'old' potatoes
(e.g. Golden Wonders or Kerr's Pinks)
1 egg, beaten
30–55g/1–2oz/¼–½ stick butter
2tablespoons/3tablespoons flour
1tablespoon/1½tablespoons chopped parsley,
   chives and lemon thyme, mixed (optional)
creamy milk
salt and freshly ground pepper
seasoned flour
bacon fat or butter for frying

1 Boil the potatoes in their jackets, pull off the skins and mash straight away.
2 Add the egg, butter, flour and herbs (if using) and mix well. Season with plenty of salt and pepper, adding a few drops of creamy milk if the mixture is too stiff.
3 Shape into a 2.5cm/1inch-thick round and then cut into eight pieces. Dip in seasoned flour.
4 Bake on a griddle over an open fire or fry in bacon fat or melted butter on a gentle heat. Cook the fadge until crusty and golden on one side, then flip over and cook on the other side (about 4–5 minutes on each side).
5 Serve with an Ulster fry or on its own on hot plates with a blob of butter melting on top.

Hay Making

I remember jogging backwards and forwards on the back of a hay cart on the way home from the fields to the haggard. It seems quite extraordinary now to think that a hay cart was still horse-drawn even in the sixties. I lived in a country village in the Irish Midlands and haymaking was one of the high points of the year when the whole community helped each other to gather the hay, with workers moving from farm to farm as they did for the harvest.

As children we were welcome in every house and adored all the excitement. We raced into the fields after school, flinging our satchels into the headlands. The boys were full of importance helping to make the haystacks but I would rush into the farm kitchen to help with the tea. Spotted Dog and apple or rhubarb cake were the standard fare and I was sometimes allowed to peel the apples or chop the rhubarb or best of all roll out the trimmings of pastry. As soon as everything was baked, great big teapots of strong tea were brewed and poured into a tin can with a lid or into whiskey bottles which were then wrapped in several layers of newspaper.

Haymaking, like harvesting, was thirsty work, so we always got a great welcome. Everyone gathered and, sitting up against a haystack, drank hot sweet tea and ate thick slices of warm fruit bread smothered with country butter, followed by apple cake.

32

Fraughan Fool with Sweet Biscuits (page 38)

Spiced Beef (page 57)

Irish Apple Cake

A traditional Irish recipe which
would originally have been
baked in an iron bastible or
pot oven beside an open fire.

serves 6
225g/8oz/2cups
   white flour
¼teaspoon baking powder
115g/4oz/1stick butter
125g/4½oz/generous
   ½cup caster sugar
1 egg, beaten
50–100ml/2–4fl oz/¼–½cup milk
2–3 Bramley cooking apples, peeled, cored and
   chopped
2–3 cloves (optional)
1 egg beaten with a pinch of salt, to glaze

1 Sieve the flour and baking powder into a bowl
and rub in the butter. Add about two-thirds (85g/
3oz) of the sugar, the egg, and enough milk to form
a soft dough.
2 Divide in two. Put one half on to a greased
ovenproof plate and pat out with floured fingers to
cover the plate.
3 Arrange the chopped apples and the cloves on
the dough and sprinkle with the rest of the sugar,
depending on the sweetness of the apples.
4 Roll out the remaining dough and cover the top.
(This is easier said than done as the dough is like a
scone dough and is very soft.) Press the sides
together, cut a slit through the lid, brush with egg
wash and bake for about 40 minutes in a 180°C/
350°F/gas4 oven.
5 Dredge with caster sugar and serve with soft
'~own sugar and softly whipped cream.

Spotted Dog

This is the traditional Irish fruit bread, also called
Sweet Cake, Currnie Cake, Spotted Dick or Railway
Cake depending on the area.

450g/1lb/4cups plain white flour
2teaspoons sugar
½teaspoon salt
½teaspoon bicarbonate of soda, sieved
85–110g/3–4oz/½cup sultanas, raisins or currants
300–350ml/10–11fl oz/1¼–1½cups sour milk or
   buttermilk
1 egg (optional – you will not need all the milk if
   you use the egg)

1 Sieve the dry ingredients, add the fruit and mix
well.
2 Make a well in the centre and add the egg if you
are using it, and most of the milk. Using one hand,
mix in the flour from the sides of the bowl, adding
more milk if necessary. The dough should be
softish, but not too wet and sticky. When it all
comes together, turn it out on to a floured board
and knead lightly for a few seconds – just long
enough to tidy it up.
3 Pat the dough into a round about 4cm/1½inches
deep and cut a deep cross in it (to let the fairies
out!). Let the cuts go over the sides of the bread.
4 Bake in a preheated 230°C/450°F/gas8 oven for
15 minutes, then turn down the oven to 200°C/
400°F/gas6 and bake for a further 30 minutes or
until cooked. If you are in doubt, tap the bottom: if
it is cooked it will sound hollow.
5 Serve freshly baked, cut into thick slices and
spread with butter.

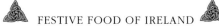

Lughnasa

The festival of Lughnasa (the Irish word for 'August') was celebrated on the first weekend of the month. It was the most joyous of the great quarterly Celtic festivals, Imbolc, Bealtaine and Samhaine being the others. Lughnasa was above all a celebration of the harvest. At last, after a long 'Hungry July', the potatoes were ready to be dug. They were boiled in the big black iron three-legged pot over the open fire, and eaten with lashings of country butter or mashed with boiled cabbage, leeks, scallions or wild garlic.

As the weather was usually good at this time of year it was the tradition in many places for entire communities to take off to a chosen meeting place in the mountains, beside a lake or stream or near a holy well for a carefree outdoor gathering. Bonfires were lit and the day was spent feasting, picking fraughans or wild raspberries, singing, dancing and engaging in all sorts of sports. There are even records of horse swimming races!

Kerry Pies

Mutton pies, made in Kerry, were served at the famous Puck Fair in Killorglin in August and taken up the hills where men were herding all day. The original hot water crust pastry was made with mutton fat but we have substituted butter for a really delicious crust.

serves 6
450g/1lb boneless lamb or mutton (from shoulder or
    leg – keep bones for stock)
275g/9½oz diced onions
275g/9½oz diced carrots
2tablespoons/3tablespoons flour
300ml/½pint 1¼cups mutton or lamb stock
1teaspoon chopped parsley
1teaspoon thyme leaves
salt and freshly ground pepper

Pastry
350g/12oz/3cups white flour
pinch of salt
170g/6oz/1½ sticks butter
100ml/4fl oz/½cup water
1 egg beaten with a pinch of salt, to glaze

1 Trim off all surplus fat, saving the scraps, then cut the meat into small neat pieces about the size of a small sugar lump.

2 Render down the scraps of fat in a hot, wide saucepan until the fat runs. Discard the pieces. Toss the diced vegetables in the fat and cook for 3–4 minutes. Remove and toss the meat in the fat over a high heat until the colour turns.

3 Stir the flour into the meat. Cook gently for 2 minutes and gradually blend in the stock. Bring to the boil, stirring occasionally. Return the vegetables to the pan with the parsley and thyme leaves, season with salt and pepper and leave to simmer, covered, until the rest is almost cooked. If using young lamb, 30 minutes will be sufficient; an older animal may take up to 1 hour.

4 Meanwhile make the pastry. Sieve the flour and salt into a mixing bowl and make a well in the centre. Dice the butter into a saucepan with the water and bring to the boil. Pour the liquid all at once into the flour and mix together quickly; beat until smooth. At first the pastry will be too soft to handle but as it cools it will become more workable. Roll out two thirds to 2.5mm/⅛–¼inch and line a 23cm/9inch pie tin (or smaller, individual pie tins).

5 Fill the pastry-lined tins with the slightly cooled meat mixture. Make lids from the remaining pastry, brush the edges of the base with water and egg wash and put on the pastry lids, pinching them tightly together. Roll out the trimmings to make pastry leaves or twirls to decorate the tops of the pies, make a hole in the centre and egg-wash carefully.

6 Bake the pie or pies at 200°C/400°F/gas6 for about 40 minutes. Serve hot or cold.

Fraughan Fool with Sweet Biscuits

Fraughans, herts or bilberries are the names used in different parts of Ireland for the intensely flavoured wild blueberries that grow on the acid hilltop soil. They were traditionally picked on the first Sunday of August – during Lughnasa – and eaten mashed with sugar or in pies. If they were plentiful they were also made into jams.

fraughans
caster (fine) sugar
whipped cream

1 Crush the berries with a pounder or potato masher and sweeten to taste with caster sugar.
2 Fold in about half their volume of whipped cream. Taste and add a little more if necessary.
3 Chill and serve with sweet biscuits.

Sweet Biscuits

170g/6oz/1½cups flour
115g/4oz/1stick butter
55g/2oz/¼cup caster (fine) sugar

1 Rub the butter into the flour and add the sugar, as for shortcrust pastry. Gather the mixture together and knead lightly.
2 Roll out to 5mm/¼inch thick and cut into rounds with a 6.5cm/2½inch cutter or into heart shapes.
3 Bake in a 180°C/350°F/gas4 oven until pale brown – about 15 minutes. Remove and cool on a rack. Serve with fruit fools, compôtes and ice creams.

38

Threshing

Nowadays rural communities rarely come together to help each other in the way that was necessary in times gone by when the harvesting was done with a binder and threshing machine. First the reaper and binder would rumble into the field around mid-August, cut the barley, wheat or oats, bind the stooks and spit them out so that they could be built into cornstacks. After a few weeks of drying out, these were brought into the haggard and built into huge hay ricks to await the day when it was the farmer's turn to have the threshing machine and elevator. On that morning twenty or more men on foot or bicycle would arrive from neighbouring farms anticipating a hard but exhilarating day's work, piking sheaves, clearing chaff and filling sacks. As this was dry, thirsty work, one of the great attractions was the barrel of beer or porter that was set up in a shed in the haggard so that the men could refresh themselves at regular intervals.

The farmer's wife, mother, sisters, cousins and several neighbours would have been hard at work since dawn baking and cooking a gargantuan dinner for the men who were fed in relays over a period of several hours. Farmers' wives vied with each other to produce the best 'feed'. Large establishments would have huge roasts of beef or lamb with lashings of roast potatoes, gravy and vegetables, whereas humbler farmers might serve bacon and cabbage or pig's head – always with copious quantities of potatoes and mugs of milk. Apple or rhubarb tarts with big mugs of hot sweet tea would round off the meal.

Irish Stew

This stew would originally have been made in a big black iron pot over the open fire. There's always great controversy in Ireland about whether there should be carrots in it or not. If you have them, put them in because they certainly improve the flavour! Some people add a parsnip or some chunks of swede or turnip, depending on the time of year.

serves 4–6
1.15–1.35kg/2½–3lb mutton or lamb chops (gigot or rack) not less than 2.5cm/1inch thick
12 baby or 5 medium carrots
12 baby or 5 medium onions
1 parsnip (optional)
½ swede or turnip (optional)
575ml/1pint/2½cups stock (lamb if possible) or water
8 potatoes (or more if you like)
sprig of thyme
1 tablespoon/1½ tablespoons roux (optional)
salt and freshly ground pepper
1 tablespoon/1½ tablespoons each of freshly chopped parsley and chives, to garnish

1 Cut the chops in half and trim off some of the excess fat. Set aside. Render down the fat on a gentle heat in a heavy pan, discarding the pieces.
2 If the carrots are young and the onions small, leave them whole. Otherwise prepare and cut them into chunks, along with the parsnips and turnips.
3 Toss the meat in the hot fat until it is slightly browned, then quickly toss the vegetables too.
4 Build the meat and vegetables up in layers in a large casserole, carefully seasoning each layer with salt and pepper.
5 Deglaze the pan with mutton stock and pour into the casserole.

6 Peel the potatoes and lay them on top of the casserole so that they will steam while the stew cooks. Season the potatoes.

7 Add the sprig of thyme, bring to the boil on top of the stove, cover and transfer to a 190°C/375°F/gas5 oven, or allow to simmer on top of the stove, until the stew is cooked – about 1–1½ hours, depending on whether the stew is being made with lamb or mutton.

8 When the stew is cooked, pour off the cooking liquid, degrease it and reheat in another saucepan. If you wish, thicken slightly by whisking a little roux into the boiling liquid. Check seasoning and pour back over the stew.

9 Bring back up to boiling point, sprinkle with chopped parsley and chives and serve from the pot or in a large pottery dish.

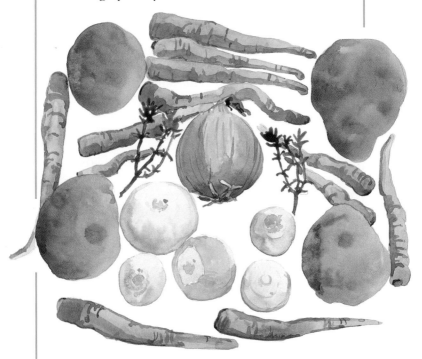

Rhubarb Tart

serves 8–12
Pastry
225g/8oz/2sticks butter
55g/2oz/¼cup caster (fine) sugar
2 eggs
350g/12oz/3cups flour

Filling
450g/1lb red rhubarb
175g/6½oz/¾cup sugar
1 beaten egg with pinch of salt, to glaze

1 First make the pastry. Cream the butter and sugar together and then add the eggs and beat for several minutes. Mix in the flour, little by little, to form a stiff dough. Chill for at leat 1 hour, otherwise the pastry will be difficult to handle.
2 Roll out half the pastry to about 3mm/⅛inch thick and line a rectangular tin or plate measuring 18cm/7inches x 30.5cm/12inches.
3 Slice the rhubarb into 1cm/½inch rounds, fill the tart and sprinkle with the sugar.
4. Roll the remaining pastry, cover the rhubarb and seal the edges. Decorate with pastry leaves, paint with egg wash and bake in a preheated 180°C/350°F/gas4 oven until the tart is golden and the rhubarb is soft (45 minutes to 1 hour).
5 When cooked cut into squares, sprinkle lightly with caster sugar and serve with softly whipped cream and Barbados sugar.
Note: This tart could also be filled with Bramley apples, gooseberries or Worcesterberries.

Michaelmas

Michaelmas, known in Ireland as Fomhar na nGeanna, falls on September 29, the feast of St Michael the Archangel. It is commonly associated with geese because the birds that we hatched in spring and put out to grass in May and on to the stubble after the harvest are plump and ready for market at this time.

Years ago most farms in Ireland would have reared geese. I have vivid childhood memories of the preparations for the Michaelmas feast in a neighbour's house. The bird was smothered several days ahead and hung by the neck in the larder. It was then plucked in an open shed. The wings were kept (and much sought after for brushing out dusty corners), the large feathers were sometimes made into quills or fishing floats, and the smaller ones and the precious down were collected for stuffing pillows and feather beds.

The goose was stuffed with potato, onion and sage stuffing and roasted slowly – by which time we would be in a fever of anticipation. Every now and then the fat would be poured off; some was used to roast potatoes but the rest was stored for myriad purposes apart from cooking – it was rubbed into chests as a remedy for wheeziness, rubbed in to the range to give it a shine or even into leather shoes. Nothing was wasted!

In many parts of the country the first corn of the new year was ground into flour and baked into bread to go with the feast and the last sheaf of wheat was the centrepiece on the table. There were many traditions attached to the last sheaf; in some places the girl who tied it had the honour of being led on to the dance floor by the farmer's son for the first dance of the evening.

Michaelmas was also the time to pick apples, so

the goose was always served with apple sauce and often followed by baked apples or a golden apple tart dusted with caster sugar.

Michaelmas Goose with Potato Apple Stuffing

serves 8–10

1 goose, weighing about 4.5kg/10lb (with giblets – neck, heart and gizzard)
1 small onion
1 carrot
bouquet garni consisting of 1 sprig of thyme, 3 or 4 parsley stalks, a small piece of celery
6 or 7 peppercorns
roux if desired for thickening

Stuffing
900g/2lb potatoes
55g/2oz/½stick butter
450g/1lb onions, chopped
450g/1lb Bramley cooking apples, peeled and chopped
1tablespoon/1½tablespoons chopped parsley
1tablespoon/1½tablespoons lemon balm
salt and freshly ground pepper

Apple Sauce (page 53)

1 First make the stuffing. Boil the unpeeled potatoes in salted water until cooked, peel and mash.
2 Melt the butter and sweat the onions in a covered saucepan on a gentle heat for about 5 minutes.
3 Add the apples and cook until they break down into a fluff, then stir in the mashed potatoes and herbs. Season with salt and pepper. Allow to get quite cold before stuffing the goose.

4. Gut the goose and singe if necessary. Remove the wishbone for ease of carving. Put the goose into a saucepan with the giblets, onion, carrot, bouquet garni and peppercorns. Cover with cold water, bring to the boil and simmer for about 2 hours. (The wing tips may also be added to the stock if desired.)

5 Remove the bird from the stock and pat dry. Season the cavity with salt and pepper and fill with the cold stuffing. Sprinkle some sea salt over the breast and rub into the skin. Roast for 2 – 2½ hours in a preheated 180°C/350°F/gas4 oven. Pour off the excess fat three or four times during the cooking (and store this fat in your refrigerator as it keeps for months and is wonderful for roasting or sautéeing potatoes). To test whether the goose is cooked, prick the thigh at the thickest part. The juices that run out should be clear; if they are pink the goose needs a little longer. When cooked remove the goose to your best large serving dish and put it into a low oven while you make the gravy.

6 To make the gravy, pour or spoon off the remainder of the fat. Add about 575ml/1pint/ 2½cups of strained giblet stock to the roasting tin, bring to the boil and, using a small whisk, scrape the tin well to dissolve the meaty deposits. Taste for seasoning and if you wish thicken with a little roux. If the gravy is weak, boil for a few minutes to concentrate the flavour; if too strong add a little water or stock. Strain and serve.

7 Bring the goose to the table, carve and serve apple sauce and gravy separately.
Note: a goose looks enormous but it has a large carcase. Allow at least 450g/1lb uncooked weight per person.

Hallowe'en

The ancient Celtic festival Samhain was celebrated
on November 1 – the first day of winter. In Christian
times the celebrations were transferred to the night
before – Hallowe'en, which is still one of the
liveliest festivals of the year. Our ancestors firmly
believed that both the fairies and the ghosts of the
dead were particularly active on this night and I well
remember as a child being told not to eat
blackberries after Hallowe'en because the devil or
púca would have spat on them.

   As children we always had a Hallowe'en party,
as many Irish children do today. We had the greatest
fun planning it for weeks before. We made black
witches' hats, scary masks and polished up our
collection of ghost stories. We tormented a local

farmer until he gave us a few turnips which we hollowed out with sharp spoons to make masks with eerie toothless grins. These were lit with stumps of candles and put up on the gate post outside the house where the party was held. On the previous day all the children participated in the making of the barmbrack, a rich fruit bread with a long history.

The word barm comes from an old English word, *beorma*, meaning yeasty fermented liquor. *Brack* comes from the Irish word *brac*, meaning speckled – which it is, with dried fruit and candied peel. Hallowe'en has always been associated with fortune telling and divination, so various objects are wrapped up and hidden in the cake mixture – a wedding ring, a coin, a pea or a thimble (signifying spinsterhood), a piece of matchstick (which means that your husband will beat you!). After dark children dress up, often as witches or ghosts in hats and masks and black shawls, light turnip lanterns in the windows and go from house to house collecting fruit and nuts.

After hours of merriment and Hallowe'en games the feast began. We ate huge plates of colcannon, a delectable Irish potato dish made with fluffy mashed potatoes, scallions and cabbage with a pool of melted butter in the centre. After that there were slices of warm apple cake (page 33) fresh from the oven with cream and soft brown sugar, and finally it was time to cut the barmbrack. Everyone longed for the ring which meant certain marriage before the year ended even if you were only five! Then the older people started to 'draw down the past' and tell ghost stories in hushed tones, into the early hours. Eventually we made our ways home clutching on to a grown-up and terrified of the least squeak – but not before we had put out a plateful of colcannon with a knob of butter in the centre for the fairies and the ghosts.

Colcannon

There are several versions of this traditional potato dish which has nourished and comforted Irish people for centuries. So popular is it that poems have been written and songs have been sung in its honour.

serves 8
900g–1kg/2–2½lb 'old' potatoes, (e.g. Golden Wonders or Kerr's Pinks)
1 small Savoy or spring cabbage (about 450g/1lb)
250ml/8fl oz/1cup milk
2tablespoons/3tablespoons chopped spring onions (or more if you like)
55g/2oz/½stick butter
salt and freshly ground pepper

1 Scrub the potatoes and leave the skins on. Put them in a saucepan of cold water, add a good pinch of salt and bring to the boil.
2 When the potatoes are about half cooked (15 minutes or so) strain off two-thirds of the water, replace the lid on the saucepan, put on to a gentle heat and allow the potatoes to steam until they are cooked.
3 Discard the dark outer leaves of the cabbage, wash the rest and cut into quarters, remove the core and cut finely across the grain. Cook in a little boiling salted water or bacon cooking water until soft. Drain, season with salt, pepper and a little of the butter.
4 When the potatoes are just cooked, put the milk into a saucepan with the scallions and bring to the boil. Pull the skins off the potatoes, mash quickly while they are still warm and beat in enough of the hot milk to make a fluffy purée. (If you have a large quantity you can do this in a food mixer.)
5 Stir in the cooked cabbage and taste for

seasoning. Colcannon may be prepared ahead up to this point and reheated later in a 180°C/350°F/gas4 oven. Cover with tinfoil before reheating so that it doesn't get crusty on top. Serve in a hot dish with a lump of butter melting in the centre.

Hallowe'en Barmbrack

A traditional fruit bread with hidden charms!

450g/1lb/4cups white flour
½level teaspoon ground cinnamon.
½teaspoon mixed spice
¼level teaspoon nutmeg
pinch of salt
55g/2oz/½stick butter
20g/¾oz yeast (or 2 teaspoons dried yeast)
85g/3oz/scant ½cup caster (fine) sugar
300ml/½pint/1¼cups tepid milk
1 egg, beaten
225g/8oz/1cup sultanas
110g/4oz/½cup currants
55g/2oz/¼cup mixed chopped candied peel

Charms
1 pea
1 ring
1 silver coin
1 short piece of matchstick,
   each wrapped in
   greaseproof paper

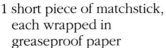

Glaze
1tablespoon/1½tablespoons sugar
2tablespoons/3tablespoons boiling water

1 Sieve the flour, spices and salt into a bowl, then
rub in the butter.
2 Cream the yeast with 1 teaspoon of the sugar and
1 teaspoon of the tepid milk; it should soon froth
slightly.
3 Pour the remaining tepid milk and the egg into
the yeast mixture and combine with the dry
ingredients and the sugar. Beat well with a wooden
spoon or knead with your hand in the bowl until the
batter is stiff but elastic.
4 Fold in the dried fruit and chopped peel, cover
the bowl with a damp cloth or pure clingfilm and
leave in a warm place until the dough has doubled
in size. Knead again for another 2–3 minutes and
divide between two greased 450g/1lb loaf tins.
5 Add the charms at this stage, making sure they are
well distributed. Cover again and leave to rise in a
warm place for about 30 minutes to 1 hour or until
the dough comes up to the top of the tin. Bake in a
preheated 180°C/350°F/gas4 oven for about 1 hour.
Test with a skewer before taking out of the oven.
6 Glaze the top with the sugar dissolved in the
boiling water. Turn out to cool on a wire tray and
when cold cut in thick slices and butter generously.
Barmbrack keeps well, but even when it's stale it is
very good toasted and buttered.

St Martin's Eve

There is a long tradition in Ireland of killing a pig on Martinmas – the eve of St Martin's Day, November 11. Originally this had pagan origins: the blood was solemnly sprinkled on the doorstep and in all four corners of the house to ward off any nasty evil spirits that might be lurking about. There were also practical reasons, of course, because pigs by now would be plump and flavourful, having fattened on mast all summer.

After the pig was butchered, some of the meat was used as fresh pork and the rest was salted and cured as bacon and stored in oak barrels where it lasted for many months. The head was salted and boiled or made into brawn. The bit I liked best as a girl was the making of the black and white puddings – wonderfully gory!

The pork fillet was usually cooked that evening, often just sliced and fried in butter. Stuffed pork steaks served with lots of Bramley apple sauce were great favourite also.

51

Roast Stuffed Pork Fillet

serves 6
2 pork fillets
salt and freshly ground pepper

Stuffing
90g/3oz/6tablespoons butter
170g/6oz chopped onion
170g/6oz/3cups soft white breadcrumbs
4tablespoons/5tablespoons freshly chopped herbs
    (parsley, thyme, chives, marjoram, savory,
    perhaps a little sage or rosemary)
salt and freshly ground pepper
or
potato and apple stuffing (use half the recipe on
    p44)
15–30g/½–1oz butter
450ml/¾pint/2 scant cups chicken stock
large needle and cotton string

1 First make the stuffing. Sweat the onions gently in
the butter for 5–6 minutes. When they are soft, stir in
the crumbs, herbs and a little salt and pepper to
taste. Allow to get quite cold.
2 Trim the pork fillets of fat and gristle. Slit each
one down one side and open out, flatten slightly
with a mallet or rolling pin and season.
3 Cover one fillet with stuffing and top with the
other fillet. Sew the edges with cotton thread.
4 Smear the top with soft butter and roast in a
200°C/400°F/gas6 oven for about 45 minutes,
depending on the size of the fillets. After 25 minutes
turn the pork over and baste so that the base
browns also.
5 When cooked transfer to a carving plate and
allow to rest while you make the gravy. Degrease
the pan juices if necessary, add the chicken stock to
the roasting pan and bring to the boil, using a whisk

to dislodge the caramelised juices from the pan. Simmer for a few minutes, taste and add seasoning if necessary. Slice the pork into thick slices, about 1cm/½inch and serve with apple sauce (see below), gravy and lots of crusty roast potatoes.

Apple Sauce

serves 8
450g/1lb cooking apples, peeled, cored and
    chopped
55g/2oz/¼cup sugar or to taste
2–4teaspoons water

Put the chopped apples in a stainless steel or cast-iron saucepan with the sugar and water, cover and cook on a very low heat until they break down into a fluff. Stir, taste for sweetness. Serve warm or cold.

Homemade Sausages

makes 16 approx
450g/1lb streaky pork
1–2 teaspoons chopped mixed herbs (thyme,
    marjoram, basil, rosemary and parsley)
1 garlic clove, crushed
1 egg, beaten
70g/2½oz/¾cup soft breadcrumbs
salt and freshly ground pepper

1 Mince the pork (twice for a smoother texture).
2 Mix the breadcrumbs with the herbs and then combine all the ingredients thoroughly. Fry a little piece of the mixture so that you can check the seasoning. Add more if necessary.
3 Fill a piping bag fitted with a 2.5cm/1inch plain nozzle. Pipe on to a floured board and cut into the required lengths. Alternatively shape by hand.
4 Fry until golden all over. Serve with apple sauce.

Christmas

Christmas in Ireland is now just as glittery and commercialised as anywhere else but in the past it was very much a family festival when sons and daughters who were working elsewhere returned for a few days. Christmas Day was spent for the most part within the home – a 'quiet Christmas' seemed to be everyone's ambition.

On Christmas morning most people went to church. In some areas boys blew cow horns or bugles at dawn to wake the neighbours for early Mass. Wisps of straw were often taken from the Christmas crib in the church to bring luck for the coming year.

After church while the womenfolk busied themselves in the kitchen with what was often the most elaborate meal of the year the men and boys would often enjoy some outdoor sport, such as hurling.

Nowadays there is hardly a household in the country that doesn't have turkey for Christmas dinner. We stuff ours with a buttery fresh herb and breadcrumb stuffing like the one on page 52. For those lucky enough to be able to get them, native Irish oysters, particularly those from Galway Bay, are a real Christmas treat. They are at their best when there is an 'r' in the month, so they are at their prime around Christmas time.

Irish Oysters

Oysters are known to be an aphrodisiac, particularly when accompanied by velvety Irish stout – even more risky than standing under the mistletoe, so beware!

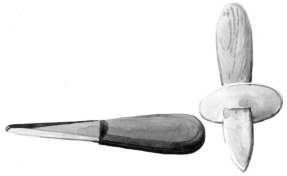

serves 2 for a feast
2 dozen native Irish oysters
seaweed
1 lemon
a little crushed ice

1 Check the oysters carefully; discard any that is even slightly open.
2 Not long before serving, open the oysters. You will need an oyster knife for this operation. Place the oyster on the worktop, deep shell down. Cover your hand with a folded tea towel and hold the oyster firmly. Put the tip of the oyster knife into the crevice at the hinge of the oyster, push hard and then quickly twist the knife. You need to exert quite a bit of pressure (hence it is essential that the hand holding the oyster is protected, in case the knife slips!). When you feel the oyster is opening, change the angle of the knife and, keeping the blade close to the shell, slice the oyster off the top shell in one movement. Then run the knife underneath the oyster in the deep shell and flip it over: be careful not to lose any of the delicious juices.
3 Put a bed of seaweed on two chilled plates, place the oysters in their shells on the seaweed and add a few fragments of lemon.
4 Serve with freshly baked brown soda bread and butter and a glass of Irish stout.

St Stephen's Day

On St Stephen's Day (Boxing Day) when I was a child there was a very old custom called Hunting the Wren which still persists in some parts of the country. Boys and girls dressed up in borrowed cast-offs and painted their faces with burnt corks or perhaps stolen lipstick then went from house to house in groups carrying a holly bush and singing the Wrenboys song.

The wren, the wren, the king of all birds
On St Stephen's Day he got caught on the furze . . .

We would be given a few pence or sometimes a bun or a few biscuits. Older groups often had several musical instruments and drove from pub to pub singing songs. The collection was usually very worthwhile because of the spirit of Christmas!

Our family tradition was tied in to the local fox hunt on St Stephen's Day. After a late breakfast we'd pack up a picnic, tumble into the car and head for the local 'hunt meet'. The picnic needed to be quite substantial because the weather was cold, and it was quite likely to be shared with many hungry friends. After the red-coated master blew his bugle to start his day's hunting he was followed not only by horses and hounds but by a stream of cars who followed the action from the nearest road.

The picnic at its most basic might include turkey and ham, spiced beef or smoked salmon sandwiches, a few wedges of Christmas cake and flasks of tea. But the real favourite was a bubbling stew transported in a haybox. This would be ladled into deep bowls and it tasted pretty terrific on a cold December day. Buttery sponge cakes, clementines, mince pies and flasks of hot mulled wine made this one of the most memorable picnics of the year.

Eventually after much good cheer everyone would gather around a blazing fire in the local pub to sip glasses of steaming hot punch.

Spiced Beef

Spiced beef is traditionally associated with St Stephen's Day (although in Cork we eat it all year round!). It may be served hot or cold and is a marvellous stand-by, because, if it is properly spiced and cooked, it will keep for several weeks in the fridge.

1.35–1.8kg/3–4lb lean flank of beef or silverside

Spice for beef
225g/8oz/1½cups demerara sugar
350g/12oz/1½cups salt
15g/½oz/2teaspoons saltpetre (available from chemists)
85g/3oz/generous ½cup whole black peppercorns
85g/3oz/generous ½cup whole allspice (pimento or Jamaican pepper)
85g/3oz/1cup juniper berries

1 Grind all the spices (preferably in a food processor) until fairly fine. The full quantity is much more than you will need for the quantity of beef given here, but it will keep for months in a screwtop jar.
2 If you are using flank remove the bones and trim away any unnecessary fat.
3 Rub the spice well over the beef and into every crevice. Put into an earthenware dish and leave in a fridge or cold larder for 3–7 days, turning occasionally. (This is a dry spice, but after a day or two some liquid will come out of the meat.) The longer the meat is left in the spice, the longer it will last and the more spicy the flavour.

4 When you are ready to cook the meat, roll and tie the joint neatly with cotton string into a compact shape. Cover with cold water and simmer for 2–3 hours or until tender and cooked.
5 If it is not to be eaten hot, press by putting it on a flat tin or into a bread tin; cover it with a board and weight and leave for 12 hours. Spiced beef will keep for 3–4 weeks in a fridge.
6 Serve cut into thin slices with some freshly made salads and home made chutneys, or use in sandwiches.

St Stephen's Day Stew

Left-over turkey and ham never taste so good as in this St Stephen's Day stew, paticularly when it is eaten out of a haybox while following the hunt on a cold winter's day.

serves 12
900g/2lb cold turkey meat
450g/1lb cold ham or bacon
30g/1oz/¼stick butter
340g/12oz chopped onions
225g/8oz flat mushrooms (or button)
900ml/32fl oz/4cups well flavoured turkey stock *or*
600ml/21fl oz/2¾cups stock and 300ml/½pint/
    1¼cups turkey gravy
150ml/5fl oz/¾cup cream
1tablespoon/1½tablespoons chopped parsley
1tablespoon/1½tablespoons chopped chives
2teaspoons fresh marjoram or tarragon if available
roux
12 hot cooked potatoes
salt and freshly ground pepper

1 Cut the turkey and ham into 2.5cm/1inch pieces.
2 Melt the butter in a wide heavy saucepan, add the chopped onions, cover and sweat for about 10

minutes until they are soft but not coloured. Remove to a large plate.

3 Meanwhile wash and slice the mushrooms. Cook over a brisk heat, a few at a time. Season with salt and pepper and add to the onions.

4 Toss the turkey and ham in the hot saucepan, using a little extra butter if necessary; add to the mushrooms and onion.

5 Deglaze the saucepan with the turkey stock, add the cream and chopped herbs. Bring to the boil, thicken with roux, add the meat, mushrooms and onions and simmer for 5 minutes. Taste and correct the seasoning.

6 Peel the freshly boiled potatoes and put on top of the stew.

7 Put the lid on the casserole, set into the haybox and cover with more hay. Serve steaming hot several hours later.

Whiskey Punch

Whiskey or *uisce beata* (meaning 'the water of life') has kept the Irish in fine high spirits since ancient times – and we certainly don't need a festival to enjoy it!

serves 1
1 measure of whiskey
2 teaspoons white sugar
4–6 cloves
2 slices fresh lemon
200ml/7fl oz boiling water

1 Put the whiskey, sugar, cloves and lemon slices into a strong glass.
2 Pour on the boiling water and stir until the sugar has dissolved.
3 Sip contentedly by a blazing fire.

The Twelfth Day of Christmas

The twelfth day of Christmas was widely known in Ireland as Nollaig na mBan – Women's Christmas. Over the festive season the men would have been pampered and eaten their fill of various meats and indeed often drunk to excess, but January 6 was the women's own feast. There would be a splendid high tea when all the dainties that the women really enjoyed were served. Thinly sliced white bread and plump sandwiches, followed by buttery scones with homemade jam and cream, then fluffy sponge cakes and tiny buns decorated with swirls of icing – and as if that wasn't enough, plum cake, gingerbread, warm apple cakes and pots of the finest tea. On January 7 the Christmas decorations were taken down and until quite recently there was a widespread custom of keeping aside the holly and wilted greenery to heat the pancake griddle on Shrove Tuesday.

Gingerbread

This is a favourite gingerbread recipe in our family. If it's not polished off immediately it will keep for ages in a tin.

makes 2 loaves
450g/1lb/4cups plain white flour
½teaspoon salt
1½teaspoons ground ginger
2teaspoons baking powder
½teaspoon bicarbonate of soda
225g/8oz/1½cups soft brown sugar
170g/6oz/1½sticks butter, cut into cubes
350g/12oz treacle
300ml/½pint/1¼cups milk
1 egg (free range if possible), beaten
1 fistful of sultanas (optional)
30g/1oz crystallized ginger, cut into 5mm/¼inch
   dice (optional)

1 Sieve all the dry ingredients together in a bowl.
2 Gently warm the brown sugar with the cubed butter, then add the treacle and milk. Allow to cool a little and stir into the dry ingredients.
3 Add the egg and sultanas and crystallized ginger if liked. Mix very thoroughly, making sure there are no lumps of flour left.
4 Divide between two lined loaf tins measuring about 23cm/9inches x 12.5cm/5inches and bake for about 1 hour in a preheated 180°C/350°F/gas4 oven.
5 Turn out of tin, cool and serve cut into thick slices and buttered.

61

Recipe Index